JOURNEY TO PASCHA

AN EXPLANATION OF THE HOLY WEEK SERVICES

JOURNEY TO PASCHA

AN EXPLANATION OF THE HOLY WEEK SERVICES

V. REV. FR. AYMAN KFOUF

ETHOS PRESS

2016

Journey to Pascha
An Explanation of the Holy Week Services

ISBN-13: 978-0692654736

Ethos Press
4940 Harroun Rd.
Sylvania, OH 43560
www.EthosPress.com

Book Cover, Layout, Graphic & Iconography Design by:
V. Rev. Father Ayman Kfouf

PRINTED IN THE UNITED STATES OF AMERICA

"Yesterday I was crucified with Him; today I am glorified with Him; yesterday I died with Him; today I am quickened with Him; yesterday I was buried with Him; today I rise with Him."

St. Gregory the Theologian

TABLE OF CONTENTS

His Eminence
The Most Reverend
Metropolitan JOSEPH

Archbishop of New York and
Metropolitan of
All North America

ANTIOCHIAN ORTHODOX CHRISTIAN ARCHDIOCESE
OF NORTH AMERICA

Christ is Risen! Indeed He is Risen!

It is with this joyful exclamation that we complete our journey through the Holy Season of Great Lent, and Holy Week. It is with this joyful exclamation that we proclaim that our Lord and God and Savior Jesus Christ has once and for all conquered death by his crucifixion and his Third-day resurrection from the dead.

We rejoice in this volume, "Journey to Pascha, An Explanation of the Holy Week Services", and we commend the efforts of the author, The Very Reverend Ayman Kfouf. Fr. Ayman has done an excellent job in capturing the beauty and solemnity of this holy season in a manner which is uplifting and approachable in its simplicity. This book gives our faithful a detailed explanation of the theological and liturgical meanings of the themes of the services of Holy Week and Pascha. The book is unique in that it incorporates iconography in the illustration and interpretation of these services. We believe that this book will be a valuable guide to help in the understanding of these services.

We bless this work by Fr. Ayman, and we encourage all who will come in contact with it to not only enjoy reading it, but to personally embrace the message of a new life in our Lord Jesus Christ.

Yours in Christ,

+Joseph
Archbishop of New York and Metropolitan of all North America

"The Resurrection of Christ is the total and definitive fulfilment of God's Covenant, in which our God becomes totally "ours" and in which we become totally "His".

+ Patriarch IGNATIUS IV

PREAMBLE

We are pleased to commend and promote this book on Holy Week and Holy Pascha by the V. Rev. Ayman Kfouf. This concise presentation exactly follows the timeline of Our Lord's Passion Week and Resurrection.

The icons which compliment the text allow us to follow Our Lord as He goes to Jerusalem on Palm Sunday and meets His destiny with all the plot and drama involved.

Here we find described in words and drawn in color, our open window where we experience, as eyewitnesses: the Pascha of the Cross where Christ as a lamb of God is sacrificed to sin as a son of God, who wins our release from its bonds; The Pascha of the Sabbath where Our Lord crosses over the shadow lands of Hades to rescue the righteous dead from the territory of the dead; and the Pascha of the Resurrection where Christ not only rescues the dead, but takes them, and us, with Him into life eternal, literally "bringing up with Him all the dead."

In Christ

+ ANTHONY
Bishop of Toledo and the Midwest

"By His Resurrection, Christ conquered sin and death, destroyed Satan's dark kingdom, freed the enslaved human race and broke the seal on the greatest mysteries of God and man."

St. Nikolai Velimirovic

INTRODUCTION

On Palm Sunday, we reach the end of the forty-day Lenten journey and enter into the most solemn and sacred week of the Church year, the Great and Holy Week.

During the Holy Week, we accompany the Lord through His most splendid, life-giving and holy journey; His journey through passion, crucifixion, death, and resurrection.

As we embrace this holy journey, it is important to remember that the services of the Holy Week are more than a plain re-enactment of the passion of Christ, His death and His resurrection; rather, they are opportunities for emotional, physical, and spiritual "sharing" and "participation" in these solemn events. Accordingly, we must share with Christ His passion, His crucifixion and His death, in order to share with Him His life-giving resurrection.

Understanding the true meaning of the liturgical and theological themes of the Holy Week and Pascha allows us to participate in these services more fruitfully and profoundly.

This booklet includes a daily guide to our journey to Pascha, and offers a simplified explanation of the theological and liturgical themes of the services of the Great and Holy Week and Pascha.

The simplified language of this guide is intended to speak to the average faithful and to help them understand the true meaning of the Holy Week services. In spite of this simplicity, however, this guide offers a complete interpretation of the vast majority of the theological and liturgical themes and practices of the Holy Week with Pascha.

The iconography used in this book is carefully selected to illustrate the theological meaning of each celebration, and to help the reader achieve a better understanding of the services, in which they participate.

V. Rev. Father Ayman Kfouf
Pascha 2016

LAZARUS SATURDAY MORNING
THE RAISING OF LAZARUS FROM THE DEAD

On this day we commemorate the raising of Lazarus from the dead. As recorded in the Gospel of St. John (11:1-45), when Jesus heard that His friend Lazarus has died, he came to his tomb and expressed His sorrow and love.

At the tomb Jesus wept, not only because His friend died, but also because humanity has lost yet another battle against death, our ultimate enemy.

When Jesus saw how tragic was the death of Lazarus on his family, he comforted them by declaring: "I am the Resurrection and the Life. He who believes in me, though he may die, yet shall he live. And whoever lives and believes in Me shall never die" (John 11:25).

Consequently, He shouted: "Lazarus, come forth!" His friend, dead for four days, walked out of the tomb.

By raising Lazarus from the dead, Jesus confirmed that death can have no dominion over Him. By raising Lazarus from the dead, Jesus affirmed that His passion, His suffering and His death on the cross will be followed by the destruction of death and the triumphant resurrection.

The raising of Lazarus from the dead is a message of reassurance and encouragement from Christ to His Disciples and to us. This message calls to mind that even when He suffers torture, crucifixion and slaughter, nevertheless, He will destroy death by His death and will grant life to all of those who believe in Him.

PALM SUNDAY MORNING
CHRIST'S TRIUMPHAL ENTRY INTO JERUSALEM

O n Palm Sunday morning we commemorate the triumphal entry of our Lord and Saviour Jesus Christ into Jerusalem (John 12:12-19).

This Sunday is called "Palm Sunday" because, according to the Gospel of St. John, when the crowd heard that Jesus was entering Jerusalem, after the raising of Lazarus, they took branches of palm trees and went forth to receive Christ (John 12:13).

A palm branch is a symbol of joy and festivity. The Jews used palm branches to welcome and honor important people, and to reward conquerors.

Consequently, the crowd gathered to welcome Jesus entering Jerusalem as the conqueror of death. To them, He conquered death by raising Lazarus. However, to Jesus, His final victory is yet to come, after His last battle against death on the cross.

On Palm Sunday, we are invited to receive Christ not only with mere palm branches (like did the Jews), but with repenting souls and humble hearts, shouting out: **"Blessed is He Who comes in the name of the Lord"** (Psalm 118:26).

DID YOU KNOW?

After the morning service of Palm Sunday, the liturgical services of the Holy Week are reversed; Orthros (the morning service) is celebrated at night and Vespers (the evening service) is celebrated in the morning. This change signifies that the Holy Week services are not merely a reenactment of historical events, but rather an *"entering into"* and *"living"* the very reality, solemnity and sanctifying nature of those events. In this manner, through Holy Week services we step out of time into eternity, and foretaste of the salvific passion, death and resurrection of Christ.

HOLY SUNDAY EVENING
BRIDEGROOM ORTHROS OF GREAT & HOLY MONDAY BY ANTICIPATION

Palm Sunday evening marks the beginning of the solemn journey of Christ toward His passion, crucifixion, death and resurrection.

The service commemorates two themes; the the prophetic figure of Joseph, son of the Patriarch Jacob, (Genesis 37-50), and the parable of the cursing of the fig tree, (Matthew 21:18-22).

While Joseph was a virtuous person, nonetheless he suffered unjustly at the hands of his brothers. However, because of his love and forgiveness, he prevailed over his adversaries and was greatly rewarded. We commemorate Joseph becuase his unjustified suffering and final triumph foreshadow the suffering of Christ and His final triumph over death, after His resurrection.

On the Great and Holy Monday, we commemorate, as well, the parable of the cursing of the fig tree (Matthew 21:18-22).

Following His entry to Jerusalem, on the way to the temple, Jesus saw a fig tree with many leaves but no fruits. Seeing that the fig tree didn't bear fruit, Jesus pronounced a curse on it, and it immediately died.

The fig tree symbolizes those Pharisees in the Synagogue, who, in hypocrisy, cared to show their outward piety and neglected the fruits of the spirit.

On Holy and Great Monday, we are invited to flee the fate of the fig tree and the hypocrisy of the unfaithful. Conversely, we are invited to acquire and bear the fruits of the spirit: *"love, joy, peace, patience, kindness, goodness, faithfulness, gentleness, self-control"* (Galatians 5:22-25).

Simultaneously, on Holy Monday, we are invited to emulate Joseph: to endure temptations, life trials and the struggles of the Fast with patience, love and forgiveness, so that we may be greatly rewarded.

THE ICON OF THE BRIDEGROOM
A BRIEF EXPLANATION

The icon of the Bridegroom portrays Christ standing half naked, wrapped in a precious crimson robe. Tilting His head in total humility and pain, He holds in His hand a rod, the symbol of His humility and suffering; it is the very rod that will be used in His beating. The rope that ties His hands symbolizes our bondage to sin, which Jesus untied through His passion, death on the cross and resurrection.

His head is crowned with a crown of thorns, symbolizing the mockery of the soldiers who *"... stripped him... platted a crown of thorns [and] put it upon his head, ...and mocked him, saying, Hail, King of the Jews! And they spit upon him, and took the reed, and smote him on the head"* (Matt 27:28-30).

The crown of thorns symbolizes, as well, the crown of the Sacrament of Marriage; and consequently it represents Christ as the Bridegroom who is eternally united with His beautiful bride, that is the Church.

The Bridegroom is depicted standing with pain and agony, with love and sacrifice, ready to embrace His journey of passion toward the cross in order to save His bride, the Church.

One of the high points of the first bridegroom service (Holy Sunday evening) is the procession with the icon of Christ the Bridegroom. The procession with the icon of the Bridegroom represents the beginning of His agonizing journey to Golgotha.

During the procession with the icon of the Bridegroom, the Bridegroom hymn is sung, calling on the faithful to prepare for the coming of the Bridegroom, "Behold, the Bridegroom cometh in the middle of the night..."

At the end of the procession, the icon is placed in the middle of the church, where it remains until Holy Thursday.

"Behold, the Bridegroom cometh in the middle of the night, and blessed is the servant whom He shall find watching, but unworthy is he whom He shall find in slothfulness. Beware, therefore, O my soul, and be not overcome by sleep; lest thou be given over to death, and shut out from the kingdom. But return to soberness and cry aloud: Holy, Holy, Holy art Thou, O God; through the Theotokos, have mercy on us." (Bridegroom Troparion)

On Holy Monday we commemorate two parables about the second coming of Christ and His last judgment: The first is the parable of the Ten Virgins (Matt. 25:1-13); the second is the parable of the Talents (Matt. 25:14-30).

The parable of the ten virgins speaks of ten virgins (bridesmaids) whose task was to receive the Bridegroom. Five virgins were prepared to receive the Bridegroom; the other five were not ready. When the Bridegroom arrived, unexpectedly in the middle of the night, only the five prepared virgins were allowed into the wedding feast; the five unprepared virgins were shut out.

According to St. Matthew, the five prepared virgins were called wise, and the unprepared virgins were called foolish. The wise virgins represent the faithful Christians, who live in vigilance and watchfulness in preparation for the second coming of Christ.

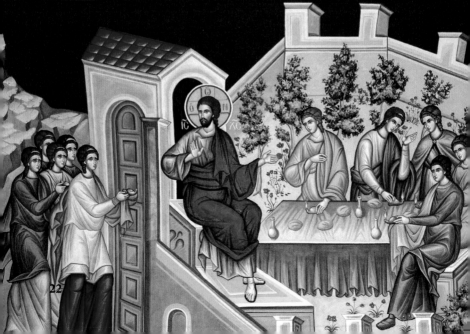

The five foolish virgins symbolize those who live in negligence and carelessness, who are concerned over earthly matters and failed to prepare for the coming of the Bridegroom "Christ".

The Second Parable, commemorated on Holy Tuesday, is the parable of the Talents (Matthew 25:14-30). The talents in the parable symbolize every good gift given by God to us. Whether we receive spiritual talents or materialistic gifts, we are responsible to wisely employ everything we have for the glory of God and the welfare of our fellow Man.

According to the Gospel of St. Matthew, the Lord will come back in His second coming to settle accounts with us and to judge us. Our judgment will be according to whether we used our talents beneficially and employed them wisely or not.

If we use our talents wisely for the glory of God, then we will be considered among God's *"trustworthy"* servants (Matthew 25:21), and will be rewarded accordingly. However, if we ignore our talents or misuse them, we will be considered among the *"wicked and lazy"* servants (Matthew 25:26), and will be judged accordingly.

On Great and Holy Tuesday, we are invited to emulate the five wise virgins and increase our spiritual vigilance and watchfulness, in preparation for the second coming of Christ and His awesome judgment.

Simultaneously, on Great and Holy Tuesday, we are invited to faithfully use our spiritual and materialistic talents for the glory of God and the welfare of others.

HOLY TUESDAY EVENING

BRIDEGROOM ORTHROS OF GREAT & HOLY WEDNESDAY BY ANTICIPATION

O n Holy Tuesday evening the Church invites us to focus our attention on two figures: the first is the sinful woman who anointed the head of Jesus with expensive ointments, in the house of Simon the leper, in Bethany (Matthew 26:6-13). The second is Judas, the disciple who betrayed Christ and surrendered Him to the hands of the transgressors.

On the one hand, by anointing the head of Christ, the sinful woman demonstrated piety and righteousness and became an example of genuine repentance and contrition of heart.

On the other hand, Judas became an example of betrayal, lack of love and despair, when he betrayed the Lord and plotted to sell Him for the love of silver.

On Holy Tuesday, we are invited to emulate the repentance of the sinful woman and ask for the forgiveness of sins.

Simultaneously, we are reminded to avoid the ingratitude and deceitfulness of Judas, and conversely to acknowledge Christ's sacrificial love and great mercy.

Before the conclusion of the service of Holy Tuesday evening, we Chant the Hymn of Kassiani, also known as the Hymn of the Sinful Woman.

Composed by Kassia, a ninth century nun-saint, the Hymn of Kassiani is an elite masterpieces of Byzantine hymnography, full of rich poetry, melodious music and theological depth. It is considered one of the highlights of the church year and the climatic conclusion of Holy Tuesday service.

The Hymn of Kassiani is based on the Gospel reading of Holy Tuesday evening (Matthew 26:6-16), which speaks of a sinful woman who anoints Jesus' head with expensive ointments.

The hymn of Kassiani invites us to acknowledge the weight of our own sins and realize our need for repentance. It assures us that with true repentance and contrition of heart, we will be granted forgiveness of sins and life eternal.

The Hymn of Kassiani

"O Lord God, the woman who had fallen into many sins, having perceived Thy divinity received the rank of ointment-bearer, offering Thee spices before Thy burial wailing and crying: "Woe is me, for the love of adultery and sin hath given me a dark and lightless night; accept the fountains of my tears O Thou Who drawest the waters of the sea by the clouds incline Thou to the sigh of my heart O Thou Who didst bend the heavens by Thine inapprehensible condescension; I will kiss Thy pure feet and I will wipe them with my tresses. I will kiss Thy feet Whose tread when it fell on the ears of Eve in Paradise dismayed her so that she did hide herself because of fear. Who then shall examine the multitude of my sin and the depth of Thy judgment? Wherefore, O my Saviour and the Deliverer of my soul turn not away from Thy handmaiden O Thou of boundless mercy"

25

HOLY WEDNESDAY EVENING
The Sacrament of the Holy Unction

On the evening of Great and Holy Wednesday, our Orthodox Church celebrates the Sacrament of Holy Unction.

Unction is a sacrament instituted by Our Lord and Savior Jesus Christ, through the teachings and practice of His disciples, for the healing of physical and spiritual ailments. *"They drove out many demons and anointed many sick people with oil and healed them"* (Mark 6:13).

The main biblical foundation for the Sacrament of Holy Unction is in the Epistle of St. James: *"Is any among you sick, let him call for the presbyters of the church, and let them pray over him, anointing him with oil in the name of the Lord; and the prayer of faith will save the sick man, and the Lord will raise him up; and if he has committed sins, he will be forgiven. Therefore, confess your sins to one another and pray for one another, that you may be healed"* (James 5:14-16).

Why?
The main purpose of this sacrament is healing; healing of the soul and body and the forgiveness of sins. The Sacrament of Unction gives the grace of God to those who suffer from ailments unto the healing of their bodies and souls.

This healing, however, is not "fairy-like", rather (as it is in all sacraments) it requires personal faith from the recipient in order for the Sacrament to truly bear fruit by the grace of God.

Who?
Traditionally, the Holy Unction service is celebrated by seven priests. Nowadays, due to practical difficulties in gathering seven priest at one service, Holy Unction can be served by one priest, and that is often the case.

When?
The liturgical service is usually served on the Great and Holy Wednesday evening, but if needed it can be served anytime during the year.

How?
The service starts with series of psalms, supplicatory hymns to God and intercessory prayers (Troparia) to the saints; followed by seven readings from the Epistles, seven readings from the Gospels and seven prayers for the sanctification of the oil.

After the conclusion of the service of the Holy Unction and the sanctification of the oil, the priest anoints the faithful with the holy oil in the form of the cross.

Traditionally the priest anoints the faithful seven times: one on the forehead, two on the cheeks, two on the hands and two on the wrists. With each anointing the priest says: *"The blessing of our Lord, God and Savior Jesus Christ: for the healing of the soul and body of the servant of God ... Amen!"*

HOLY THURSDAY MORNING
COMMEMORATION OF THE MYSTICAL SUPPER OF CHRIST
VESPERAL DIVINE LITURGY OF ST. BASIL THE GREAT

On Holy Thursday morning, we commemorate the institution of the Holy Mystery of Eucharist; the washing of disciples' feet; and the betrayal of Judas.

The Institution of the Holy Mystery of Eucharist:
While He was gathering with His disciples at the last supper, Jesus identified Himself with the bread and wine: ***"Take, eat; this is my Body. Drink of it all of you; for this is my Blood of the New Covenant"*** (Matthew 26:26-28). With these words, Christ instituted the Sacrament of the Holy Eucharist, foreshadowing His passion, sacrifice on the cross, death and resurrection. Therefore, through the Mystery of Eucharist we partake of the sacrificed, risen and most holy Body of Christ.

The Washing of the Disciples' Feet:

After revealing His divinity, through the institution of Holy Eucharist, Christ demonstrated His perfect humanity through the washing of the feet of His disciples (John. 13:2-17). The washing of the feet of the disciples illustrates Christ's perfect love and extreme humility.

In turn, we are invited to emulate Christ and show humility and love in order for us to be counted first in the Kingdom of God (Matthew 20:27-28).

The Betrayal of Judas:

After the Mystical Supper, Christ went with His disciples to the Garden of Gethsemane to pray before His journey toward the cross. In the Garden, the lawless Judas betrayed Christ with a kiss and delivered Him to be crucified.

The wretchedness of Judas resulted from the fact that he witnessed the divinity of Christ, attended the institution of the Holy Eucharist, ate the holy bread from the Lord's hands, and yet he betrayed Him.

Unlike Judas who betrayed Christ immediately after receiving the heavenly bread at the last supper, we are invited to offer the Lord thanksgiving for His love, blessings and His life-giving heavenly Eucharistic gifts.

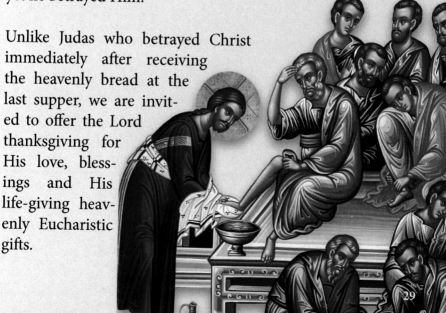

29

HOLY THURSDAY EVENING
THE SERVICE OF THE TWELVE PASSION GOSPELS
ORTHROS OF GREAT & HOLY FRIDAY BY ANTICIPATION

After witnessing the betrayal of the Lord by Judas and His capture by the soldiers to be delivered into judgment, we come on Holy Thursday evening to accompany Christ in His holy journey toward the cross.

During this service, we read the Twelve Passion Gospels, through which we hear about Christ's passion, His last instructions to the disciples, His trial in front of Pilate, His conviction, and finally His crucifixion and death on the cross.

One of the high points of this service is the procession with the crucifix around the church. After the reading of the fifth Gospel, the priest carries up the crucifix around the church in a solemn procession, while chanting the 15th antiphon: *"Today He is suspended on a Tree who suspended the earth over the waters."*

The procession with the crucifix around the church is a reenactment of the journey of Christ, carrying the cross from the gate of judgment (the place where He was judged by Pilate and was sentenced to death) up to the Golgotha or the place of the skull, where He was crucified.

After the Procession with the crucifix, the crucifix is mounted in the middle of the church, with great solemnity, to be adorned and worshiped.

The service of the Twelve Passion Gospels is a live reenactment and a mystical participation in the journey of Christ through His awesome, holy, and saving Passion: *"... the spitting, the blows with the palm of the hand, the buffeting, the mockery, the reviling, the wearing of the purple robe, the reed, the sponge, the vinegar, the nailing, the lance, and above all, the Crucifixion and Death Which He condescended to endure willingly for our sakes"* (Synaxarion for Holy and Great Friday).

HOLY FRIDAY MORNING
Royal Hours of Great & Holy Friday

The service of Royal Hours in Holy Friday consists of the daily First, Third, Sixth, and Ninth Little Hours services, combined into one office.

The service of Royal Hours (also called Great Hours) is celebrated through the reading of a set of Psalms, special hymns and scriptural readings from the Old Testament, Epistles and Gospels. Both liturgical and scriptural readings, revolve around, and reflect the significance of the theme of Great and Holy Friday: the passion, crucifixion, and death of our Lord.

The service of the Royal Hours is an opportunity for us to meditate on the holy suffering of Christ, His death and His anticipated resurrection. The service of Royal Hours brings to mind the events Jesus underwent during each of these hours.

As we progress from one hour to another, we continue to form more complete picture of the redeeming sacrifice of the Lord. By the conclusion of the service of Royal Hours, we become more aware of the solemnity and awesomeness of the events in which we participate.

Did you Know?
During the Byzantine era, it was customary for the Emperor to attend the entire service of Great Hours on Holy Friday, and for this reason, it became known as the "Royal Hours".

HOLY FRIDAY AFTERNOON
THE TAKING OF THE BODY OF JESUS DOWN FROM THE HOLY CROSS
GREAT VESPERS OF GREAT & HOLY FRIDAY

The solemn Vespers of Great Friday is celebrated in the afternoon at the time of Jesus' death. All readings from Scriptures remind us of the suffering of Christ, His passion and His death. The Old Testament readings direct our attention toward *"the Lamb that is led to the slaughter"* (Isaiah 53:7). The Epistle of Saint Paul speaks on the power and wisdom of the Cross (1 Corinthians 1:18), while the Gospel reading describes the trial of our Lord before Pilate, His crucifixion, death and burial.

One of the high points of this service is the taking of the body of Jesus down from the holy cross. During the reading of the Gospel, when the priest reaches the verse that reads: *"As evening approached, there came a rich man from Arimathea, named Joseph... Joseph took the body, wrapped it in a clean linen cloth, and placed it in his own new tomb..."* (Matthew 27:57-60), the priest and his concelebrants (if any) exit the altar through the north door, carrying a large white linen shroud, and come to stand before the cross in the middle of the church.

At this point, while the priest removes the body of Christ from the cross, the participating faithful may be invited to hold the linen shroud under the cross, and help the priest wraps the body of Christ (Matthew 27:59-60). The priest takes the body of Christ to the sanctuary and places it on the altar table.

Following the taking of the body of Jesus down from the holy cross, the procession with the holy epitaphios takes place. The holy epitaphios is a large cloth, embroidered, and richly adorned with the icon of Christ lying in the tomb.

While chanting the Aposticha (hymn), the priest carries the epitaphios above his head and makes a solemn procession from the north door of the altar to the center of the church, toward the bier of Christ. After processing three times around the bier of Christ, the epitaphios is placed inside the bier. Following, the priest places the Gospel on top of the epitaphios; then he sprinkles the epitaphios and the bier of Christ with holy and fragrant water.

At the service of the *"Taking Down of the Body of Christ from the Cross"* we participate in the salvific burial of the Lord and Saviour Jesus Christ, in anticipation of His glori- ous resurrection.

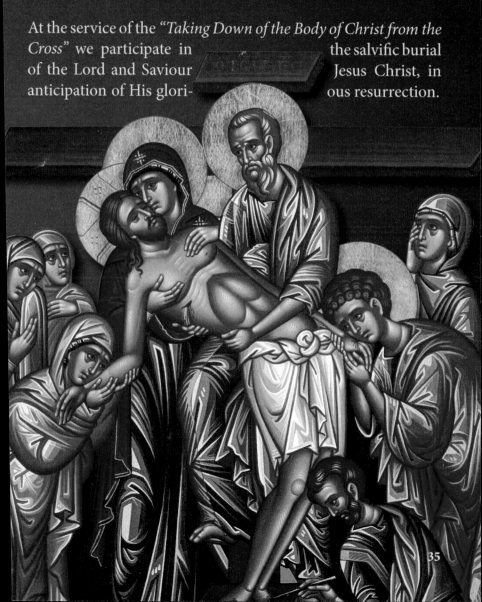

HOLY FRIDAY EVENING
THE LAMENTATION SERVICE
ORTHROS SERVICE OF SATURDAY MORNING BY ANTICIPATION

The "Lamentation Service" is a collection of short, poetic verses lamenting the passion, death and burial of Christ.

On the evening of the Holy and Great Friday, the bier of Christ is placed in the middle of the church, symbolizing the holy tomb of Christ. The epitaphios, which represents the body of Christ, is placed inside the bier and surrounded with roses and flowers.

Symbolically, as we stand in front of the tomb of Christ (the bier), singing the lamentations for His undeserved death, we simultaneously celebrate with joy His life and His victory over death.

One of the high points of this service is the procession with the bier of Christ, which takes place near the end of the service, after the Great Doxology.

The procession is made outside and around the church while singing the thrice-holy hymn, *"Holy God, Holy Mighty, Holy Immortal, have mercy on us."*

At the end of the procession, the bier of Christ is brought back to the church. Before entering into the church, the procession stops outside the doors of the church. The bier then is held above the doors, so that those who enter the church will pass underneath it, kiss the Gospel book and proceed back to the pews.

Passing under the bier of Christ, symbolizes our willingness to die with Christ in order to share His resurrection. It is a symbolic renewal of our baptismal covenant through which *"... we are buried with [Christ] by baptism into death: that like as Christ was raised up from the dead... even so we also should walk in newness of life"* (Romans 6:4).

Finally, the epitaphios (symbolizing the wrapped body of Christ) will be brought directly to the sanctuary, where it remains on the holy table until Ascension Thursday.

"My most sweet Son. I escaped sufferings and was blessed beyond at Thy strange birth. Thou who art without beginning. But now, beholding Thee, my God, dead and without breath, I am sorely pierced by the sword of sorrow. But arise, that I may be magnified" (9th Ode, Katavasia of Holy Saturday Matins).

HOLY SATURDAY MORNING

COMMEMORATING CHRIST'S VICTORY OVER DEATH & THE HARROWING OF HELL
VESPERAL DIVINE LITURGY OF ST. BASIL THE GREAT

While Christ's body is laid in the tomb, He descended with the soul into the lower parts of earth, not as a victim but as a victor. When Christ descended into hell, He destroyed the gates of hades, loosed the bonds of death and chained Satan.

When the gatekeepers of hell saw Christ, they fled; the bronze gates were broken open, and the iron chains [of hades] were undone." (St. Cyril of Alexandria)

When Christ *"descended into the lower parts of the earth"* (Ephesians 4:9), He announced His resurrection to the dead and saved them from the captivity of Satan.

"The voice of our Lord sounded into Hell, and He cried aloud and burst the graves one by one. Trembling took hold on Death when angels brought out the dead to meet Christ, who was dead and gives life to all." (St. Cyril of Alexandria).

38

On Holy and Great Saturday morning our sorrow is being transformed into joy, the joy of the anticipated resurrection of Christ. At the service, we express this joyful anticipation in the resurrection of Christ through the scattering of rose petals and bay leaves, while singing: *"Arise, O God, judge the earth; for thou shall inherit all the nations"* (Prokeimenon 'Hymn' of Great Saturday).

"Today Hades groaned, crying: My power hath vanished, because I received [Christ] as one of the dead, but I could not hold him completely. Rather, I lost with Him those who were under my reign, [when He] raised all" (Holy Saturday Vespers).

HOLY SATURDAY EVENING
GREAT & HOLY PASCHA
MIDNIGHT OFFICE, THE RUSH SERVICE & ORTHROS OF PASCHA

Finally, on Saturday night, we reach the highpoint of our lenten journey and come to celebrate the life-giving resurrection of our Lord.

The "Rush Service" begins in complete darkness, symbolizing the darkness of the grave and the darkness of creation before the resurrection of Christ. In the middle of darkness, the priest takes the lit candle from the altar and comes out among the people proclaiming, *"Come, take light from the Light that is never overtaken by night..."* The faithful proceed to light their candles, and then all begin the procession outside of the church.

Outside of the church, the priest and the people stand in front of the closed doors of the church, symbolizing the sealed tomb of Christ. Then the priest reads the Gospel according to St. Mark (16:1-8), proclaiming the resurrection of Christ, *"He is not here. He is risen as He said."*

Hearing the proclamation of the empty tomb and the announcement of the resurrection of Christ, we immediately shout singing with joy: *"Christ is risen from the dead, trampling down death by death, and upon those in the tomb bestowing life."*

The doors of the church open and the faithful proceed back to the church to start the celebration of the holy and glorious Pascha.

"Pascha" is the traditional Greek name of the feast of Easter in the Orthodox Church. Pascha means Passover: the mystical Passover from death unto life and from earth unto heaven.

Pascha is the feast of feasts and the season of seasons. In Pascha we celebrate the resurrection of Christ from the dead, and consequently our own resurrection from the death of sin.

The thematic proclamation of the Paschal services is **"Christ is Risen!"** is a proclamation of faith that forms the foundation of every aspect of our Orthodox and Christian life, *"... if Christ has not been raised, then our preaching is in vain and your faith is in vain"* (1 Cor 15:14).

On Great and Holy Pascha, we do not only commemorate the historical event of the resurrection of Christ, but rather we come as "*participants*" in His passion, death and consequently His resurrection.

The resurrection of Christ is the first fruit of the resurrection of all humanity, and the fulfillment of the promise of our personal resurrection and eternal life.

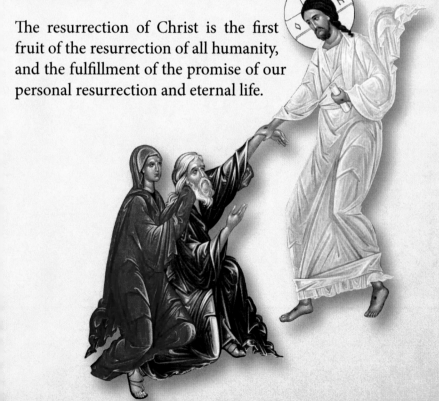

PASCHA SUNDAY MORNING
AGAPE VESPERS OF THE HOLY & GLORIOUS PASCHA

Icon painted by Duccio Di Buoninsegna 1308-1311

O n Pascha (Easter) Sunday noon, we gather, again, in the church to continue our Paschal celebration with the Agape Vespers, or the Paschal Vespers. We come to celebrate the gift of life that Christ granted to us through His life-giving resurrection. The victory of Christ over death becomes our personal victory over the death of sin and iniquity.

During the service of the Paschal Agape Vespers, just before the Gospel reading, we sing the Great Prokeimenon: ***"Who is so great a God as our God? Thou art the God who workest wonders,"*** declaring the greatness of our risen Lord. How great is our Lord? Whose suffering became the source of our joy; Whose crucifixion became the source of our liberation; and Whose death became the source of our life.

One of the high points of the service of Agape Vespers is the reading of the Gospel according to St. John (20:19-25) in various languages. The reading of the Gospel in various languages symbolizes the Church's mission to proclaim the good news of the resurrection of Christ to all nations.

The icon (left) depicts the first appearance of Christ to the disciples while they were meeting in Jerusalem. In the icon, the disciples raise their hands in fear and astonishment as they watched Christ entered the room while the doors were shut (John 20:19). Christ is depicted in a gesture of comforting and assuring: *"Peace be with you"*, He said, to pacify the souls of His disciples and to take away their fear.

The icon clearly shows the signs of crucifixion on Christ's hands, which assured the disciples that they were seeing the risen Lord Himself in His glorified body, *"He showed unto them His hands and His side. Then were the disciples glad when they saw the Lord"* (John 20:20).

Before Christ left, He bestowed upon His disciples the Holy Spirit, which will be their aid in preaching the Gospel of the resurrection to the whole world.

In turn, we are also commissioned to preach the good news of the resurrection of the Lord to the whole world. Therefore, we gather on Pascha Sunday to celebrate the resurrection of Christ; call to mind His first appearance to the disciples through which He confirmed the truthfulness of His resurrection; and to acknowledge our commission to preach the Gospel to the whole world.

THE EASTER EGG
A Symbol Of Christ's Resurrection

The Easter egg represents the sealed tomb of Christ, where He was placed after His death on the cross. The metaphor of this comparison is that: in the same way as the hard shell of the newly-hatched egg is broken open in order for a new life to start, similarly, the sealed tomb of Christ broke open after His three-day resurrection, granting new life to mankind. For this reason, the Ester egg is used in the church as a symbole of the resurrection of Christ.

According to tradition, after the crucifixion and resurrection of Christ, Saint Mary Magdalene was brought in front of the Emperor of Rome, Tiberius Caesar, in the presence of a large crowd.

St. Mary began talking to the Emperor about the resurrection of Christ. St. Mary presented to the Emperor an egg to illustrate her point about the resurrection. Caesar, then, interrupted her and replied: *"This is impossible to believe."* He added: *"there is more chance of the egg that you hold to turn red in your hands than there is a chance of Christ returning to life after He died."*

Immediately, the egg turned red in her hand.

It is because of this tradition; Easter eggs are dyed red in the Orthodox Church.

St. Mary Magdalene before the Roman Emperor, 19th Century Icon, Jerusalem

The icon (above) is a nineteenth century icon, written by the Russian artist Sergei Ivanov (1864-1910). The icon is located in the Orthodox Church of St. Mary Magdalene, on the Mount of Olives, near the Garden of Gethsemane in East Jerusalem.

The icon, which hangs above the iconostasis of the church, shows St. Mary Magdalene before the Roman Emperor, Tiberius Caesar, holding in her hand a red egg which miraculously turned red in front of the Emperor.

THE BRIGHT WEEK

During the early centuries of Christianity, the Church designated Holy Saturday for the baptism of the catechumens. Catechumens were a class of pagans and Jews who were taught the Christian faith in preparation for their baptism on Holy Saturday.

In the early church, baptism was not an individual family event, as it became today. Rather, baptism was a communal celebration of the whole Church.

For this reason, catechumens were baptized in groups, dressed in white robes and received into the Divine Liturgy on Holy Saturday, while the choir sang: *"As many as have been baptized unto Christ, have put on Christ."*

Traditionally, all newly baptized catechumens would wear white robes for the seven following days of Pascha. The white robe, worn after baptism, symbolizes the garment of light and righteousness, which is granted to the newly baptized. For this reason, this week became know as the "Bright Week."

46

The Bright Week is considered as a continuation of the Paschal celebration, therefore all services during this week are identical to the service of Pascha, with very few changes. During the Bright Week there is no fasting on Wednesdays and Fridays, due to the fact that there is no place for the mournful element of fasting during the week of light, the week of the resurrection of Christ.

Today, with the absence of the collective baptism of catechumens, we still celebrate the Bright Week as a remainder that the Resurrection of Christ is a historical event that took place in a certain time, a certain place and followed certain traditions.

We celebrate the Bright Week in remembrance of the renewal of our own baptismal garment and the illumination of our souls.

We celebrate the Bright Week in remembrance of the shining light of the resurrection of Christ in our souls, and our participation –through grace– in the light that is never taken by night.

PASCHAL GREETING

The "Paschal Greeting" is the traditional salutation of Pascha (Easter) in the Orthodox Church. The Paschal greeting is used in the Paschal season, which begins with Pascha and ends with the feast of the Ascension of Christ.

As Orthodox Christians, we replace our everyday greeting "Hello, Hi, Hey…" with the Paschal Greeting: "Christ is Risen! Indeed, He is Risen!" The faithful greet one another with "Christ is Risen!", and respond with "Indeed, He is Risen!"

The "Pascal Greeting" isn't only a simple salute, rather it is a confession of faith. Every time we greet each other with "Christ is Risen! - Indeed, He is Risen!", we affirm our faith in the resurrection of Christ and His triumph over death. (Matt 27:64, 28:6–7, Mark 16:6, Luke 24:6, 24:34).

ENGLISH: "Christ is risen! Indeed, He is risen!"

ARABIC: "المسيح قام! حقا قام!"
(al-Maseeh qām! Haqqan qām!)

GREEK: "Χριστὸς ἀνέστη! Ἀληθῶς ἀνέστη!"
(Khristós anésti! Alithós anésti!)

RUSSIAN: "Христос воскресе! Воистину воскресе!"
(Khristos voskrese! Voistinu voskrese!)

SERBIAN: "Христос васкрсе! Ваистину васкрсе!"
(Khristos vaskrse! Vaistinu vaskrse!)

LATIN: "Christus resurrexit! Resurrexit vere!"

ITALIAN: "Cristo è risorto! È veramente risorto!"

SPANISH: "Cristo ha resucitado! En verdad ha resucitado!"

ROMANIAN: "Hristos a înviat! Adevărat a înviat!"

Made in the USA
Middletown, DE
17 February 2020